First published 2024 by The O'Brien Press Ltd.,
12 Terenure Road East, Rathgar, Dublin 6, D06 HD27, Ireland.
Tel: +353 1 4923333; Fax: +353 1 4922777
E-mail: books@obrien.ie
Website: obrien.ie
The O'Brien Press is a member of Publishing Ireland.

978-1-78849-488-5

Copyright for text, typesetting, layout, design © The O'Brien Press Ltd.
Translation by Patricia Nic Eoin. **www.allaboutirish.ie**
Design by Emma Byrne
Cover image by Shutterstock

All rights reserved. No part of this publication may be reproduced or uti-
lised in any form or by any means, electronic or mechanical, including for
text and data mining, training artificial intelligence systems, photocopying,
recording or in any information storage and retrieval system, without
permission in writing from the publisher.

10 9 8 7 6 5 4 3 2 1
28 27 26 25 24

Printed and bound in Poland by Bialostockie Zaklady Graficzne S.A.
The paper in this book is produced using pulp from managed forests.

Published in:

The

Little Book o

Celtic

Mindfulness

THE O'BRIEN PRESS
DUBLIN

Introduction

*'There is no language like the Irish for
soothing and quieting.'*

So said our beloved writer J.M. Synge. And where
better to find that calm than in the profound
wisdom of Celtic proverbs on nature, wellbeing,
what it means to be human, and the very essence
of life itself.

With this book, think of each page as its own
mindful moment. These age-old sayings bring
home the power of patience and trusting the
process, of a belief in the good of others and
finding our strength within. They are valuable
reminders that inspiration is all around us,
helping us to slow down and celebrate the now.

So take a few minutes to be still, notice the
world around you, and bring a little Celtic
mindfulness into your life.

De réir a chéile a thógtar na caisleáin.

Little by little are
castles built.

Ní neart go cur le chéile.

There's no strength
like unity.

Bíonn siúlach scéalach.

They who travel have
stories to tell.

Giorraíonn beirt bóthar.

Two shorten the road.

Níor bhris focal maith
fiacail riamh.

A good word never
broke a tooth.

Is fearr an tsláinte ná
na táinte.

Health is better
than wealth.

Mol an óige agus tiocfaidh sí.

Praise the young and
they will flourish.

Is maith an t-anlann an t-ocras.

Hunger is the best
sauce.

Is binn béal ina thost.

A mouth in silence
is sweet.

Bíonn blas ar an mbeagán.

A little tastes best.

*Ní dhéanfaidh smaoineamh
an treabhadh duit.*

You'll never plough a field by turning it over in your mind.

An donas amach is an sonas isteach.

Out with the bad and
in with the good.

Tús maith leath na hoibre.

A good start is half
the work.

Ní bhíonn in aon rud

ach seal.

Nothing lasts forever.

Is fada an bóthar nach mbíonn casadh ann.

It's a long road that
has no turning.

Is olc an ghaoth nach séideann do dhuine éigin.

It's an ill wind that
blows no good.

Cleachtadh a dhéanann máistreacht.

Practice makes
mastery.

Níl aon tinteán mar
do thinteán féin.

There's no hearth like your own hearth.

An rud is annamh is iontach.

What's seldom is
wonderful.

Ní féidir ceann críonna a chur ar cholainn óg.

You can't put an old head on young shoulders.

Leagfaidh tua bheag

crann mór.

A small axe will fell a
big tree.

*Maireann croí éadrom
i bhfad.*

A light heart
lives long.

Ní bhíonn an rath ach mar a mbíonn an smacht.

There is no success without discipline.

*Filleann an feall ar
an bhfeallaire.*

Treachery rebounds
on the treacherous.

Is fearr clú ná conách.

A good name is more important than wealth.

Is maith an scathán
súil charad.

A friend's eye is a good mirror.

Is fearr obair ná caint.

Action is better
than talk.

Is maith an scéalaí an aimsir.

Time is a good
storyteller.

Dá fhada an lá, tagann an tráthnóna.

No matter how long
the day, evening
comes.

Ní huasal ná íseal,
ach thuas seal is thíos seal.

Neither noble nor lowly, but up a while and down a while.

Ar scáth a chéile a mhaireann na daoine.

It is in each other's shelter that people live.

Is glas iad na cnoic
i bhfad uainn.

Distant hills
are green.

Is trom an t-ualach
an t-aineolas.

Ignorance is a heavy burden.

Is fearr lúbadh ná briseadh.

It's better to bend
than to break.

Ná caill do mhisneach.

Don't lose your
courage.

Bíonn gach tús lag.

All beginnings
are weak.

An áit a mbíonn an dólás,
bíonn an sólás ina aice.

Where there is sorrow,
solace is nearby.

Is geal leis an bhfiach dubh
a ghearrcach féin.

Its own chick is bright
to the raven.

Ní bhíonn saoi gan locht.

There is no wise
person without fault.

Aithnítear cara i gcruatan.

A friend is recognised
in hardship.

Is fearr rith maith ná drochsheasamh.

A good run is better
than a bad stand.

An té a chuireann san earrach bainfidh sé san fhómhar.

They who plant in the spring will harvest in the autumn.

Is minic a rinne bromach gioblach capall cumasach.

It's often a poor colt
made a good horse.

Níl tuile dá mhéad
nach dtránn.

Every tide has its ebb.

Ní mar a shíltear a bhítear.

Things are not always
as they seem.

An rud atá thart,

bíodh sé thart.

What is over,
let it be over.

An rud atá i ndán duit,

ní rachaidh sé tharat.

What's for you
won't pass you.

An rud is fiú a dhéanamh,
is fiú é a dhéanamh
go maith.

That which is
worth doing is worth
doing well.

Beidh lá eile ag an bPaorach.

There will always be
another day.

Is geal le scíth malairt oibre.

A change of work is
as good as a rest.

Is trom cearc i bhfad.

A hen carried far
is heavy.

Is fearr éan i do dhorn ná péire ar an gcraobh.

A bird in the fist is
worth two on the
branch.

Feiceann súil ghruama

saol gruama.

A miserable eye sees a
miserable life.

Is fearr beagán cúnaimh
ná mórán trua.

A little bit of help is better than a lot of sympathy.

Ná bíodh do lámh i mbéal

an mhadra.

Don't tempt the dog
to bite.

Doras feasa fiafraí.

Questioning is the door to knowledge.

An croí atá i ngrá leis an
saol, is aige atá sonas
thar maoil.

The heart that loves
life is the heart
overflowing with
happiness.

Molann an obair an fear.

The work is a
testament to the
person.

Imíonn an tuirse ach fanann an tairbhe.

The tiredness leaves
but the benefit
remains.

Ní hé lá na gaoithe lá
na scolb.

A windy day is not a
day for thatching.

Is annamh earrach gan fuacht.

Seldom is Spring
without cold.

Ní féidir leis an ngobadán an dá thrá a fhreastal.

The sandpiper cannot
attend to two beaches.

Is fearr súil romhat ná dhá shúil i do dhiaidh.

One eye to the future
is better than two eyes
to the past.

An té atá sásta is duine saibhir é.

Rich is the person
who is content.

An rud atá le teacht,

tiocfaidh sé.

What is to come
will come.

*Is deacair an bua a fháil ar
an duine nach ngéillfidh
go deo.*

It's hard to beat the
one who will never
give up.

Ní peaca an dóchas.

Hope is not a sin.

*Is fearr treabhadh mall ná
gan treabhadh ar bith.*

Better to plough late
than not to plough
at all.

Is iad an codladh agus an gáire an dá leigheas is fearr.

Sleep and laughter
are the two best
medicines.

Is minic gurb é an faitíos máthair an mhisnigh.

Fear is often the
mother of courage.

Ní fhanann muir
le fear sotail.

The tide does not wait
for the arrogant.

Níor chaill fear an mhisnigh riamh.

The brave man
never lost.

Ná mol agus ná cáin tú féin.

Neither praise nor
criticise yourself.

Ná téigh san uisce mura bhfuil an snámh agat.

Do not go in the water
if you cannot swim.

Is fearr an t-aon ghníomh amháin ná céad focal.

A single deed bests a
hundred words.

Bíonn a chosán féin ag gach duine.

Everyone has their own path.

Déan rud amháin agus
déan go maith é.

Do one thing and
do it well.

Múineann gá seift.

Necessity teaches
resourcefulness.